WHO INVENTED
THE GAME?

BASED ON THE PUBLIC TELEVISION SERIES

BASEBALL™
THE · AMERICAN · EPIC

WHO INVENTED THE GAME?

BY GEOFFREY C. WARD
AND KEN BURNS WITH PAUL ROBERT WALKER

ILLUSTRATED WITH PHOTOGRAPHS

ALFRED A. KNOPF · NEW YORK

Photo credits:
Archive Photos: pages 59, 64; Associated Press/Wide World Photos: 50, 66, 67, 68, 70, 73, 74, 79; Bettmann Archive: 42 (*bottom*), 61; Cornell University/Harold Israel: 69; Crandall Library: 7; Culver Pictures: 2, 32; Freelance Photographers Guild: 57, 62; William Gladstone: 9; Historical Society of Delaware: 40; Library of Congress: 18 (*top*), 22, 23, 25, 30; Los Angeles Dodgers, Inc.: 55; Los Angeles Dodgers, Inc./Barney Stein: 49; Michael Mumby: 26, 29; National Baseball Library & Archive, Cooperstown, N.Y.: 6, 8, 13, 14, 17, 18 (*bottom*), 19, 24, 28 (*top*), 33, 36, 37 (*bottom*), 39, 43, 45, 47, 48, 51 (*top*), 52, 56, 65; *New York Daily News*: 37 (*top*); New-York Historical Society: 16; Northern Indiana Historical Society: 53; Ohio Historical Society: 41; Corey R. Shanus: 12 (*bottom*); *The Sporting News*: 27, 28 (*bottom*), 31, 42 (*top*), 60; *Sports Illustrated*/Jacqueline Duvoisin: 78; *Sports Illustrated*/Heinz Kluetmeier: 77; *Sports Illustrated*/Neil Leifer: 72; *Sports Illustrated*/Herb Scharfman: 71; Transcendental Graphics/ Mark Rucker: 10, 12 (*top*), 21, 34, 51 (*bottom*); University of Kansas: 46; University of Louisville/Hillerich & Bradsby Collection: 38; UPI/Bettmann: 75, 76; *World Telegram*: 63

THIS IS A BORZOI BOOK PUBLISHED BY ALFRED A. KNOPF, INC.

Library of Congress Cataloging-in-Publication Data
Ward, Geoffrey C.
Who invented the game? / by Geoffrey C. Ward and Ken Burns with Paul Robert Walker.
p. cm. — (Baseball, the American epic)
"Based on the public television series."
Includes index.
ISBN 0-679-86750-3 (trade) — ISBN 0-679-96750-8 (lib. bdg.)
1. Baseball—United States—History—Juvenile literature. I. Burns, Ken, 1953–
II. Walker, Paul Robert. III. Series.
GV863.A1W46 1994
796.357'0973—dc20 94-9166

Manufactured in the United States of America
2 4 6 8 0 9 7 5 3 1

CONTENTS

INNING 1
The Game Begins
6

INNING 2
Flashing Spikes and Flying Dutchmen
16

INNING 3
Gentlemen and Black Sox
24

INNING 4
The Babe
32

INNING 5
Hard Times, Good Times
40

INNING 6
Breaking the Barrier
48

INNING 7
On the Move
56

INNING 8
Mets and Other Miracles
64

INNING 9
Free Agents and Million-Dollar Men
72

INDEX
80

THE GAME BEGINS. There is a story that goes something like this: In the summer of 1839, in the small town of Cooperstown, New York, a group of schoolboys played town ball against the boys from a rival school. The rules were so loose that every hit was fair, and the players ran into each other all the time. So a Cooperstown player named Abner Doubleday created new rules for a new game—and he called it *baseball*.

This story has been told to five generations of American children. But it is not true.

LEFT: A SMALL-TOWN
TEAM IN THE 1880s.

HERE, BOYS PLAY ON
A SUMMER AFTERNOON
IN GLENS FALLS, NEW
YORK, IN THE 1890s.

No one invented baseball. But a long parade of amazing people—sluggers and sliders, saints and sinners, fireballers and flakes—made baseball the game it is today. Here's the real story.

Americans played games with bats and balls long before the Revolutionary War. At first, these sports strongly resembled the English games of cricket and rounders. Then, in 1845, a group of businessmen formed the New York Knickerbocker Base Ball Club, and led by a player named Alexander Joy Cartwright, they created new rules that still lie at the heart of modern baseball.

Town ball—the most popular of the older ball games—was a game in which pitching counted for little and scores could run into a hundred or more. The Knickerbockers' new game was more orderly and more challenging. If the batter missed three pitches, he was out; when he did get a hit, the ball was thrown to the base rather than aimed right at the runner. And though the pitcher still delivered the ball underhand, the best baseball hurlers began to challenge hitters with hard-thrown, deceptive pitches.

The new brand of baseball caught on quickly. A National

THE NEW YORK KNICKERBOCKERS *(LEFT)* AND THE BROOKLYN EXCELSIORS *(RIGHT)* POSE BEFORE A GAME IN 1858. SIXTH FROM THE LEFT IS HARRY WRIGHT, WHO LATER FORMED THE FIRST PROFESSIONAL BASEBALL TEAM.

Association of Base Ball Players formed, and by the spring of 1861, it boasted 62 clubs. But the spring season was interrupted when Confederate gunships fired on Fort Sumter and the Civil War began.

For the next four years, America was a bloody battleground as soldiers from North and South fought over the very existence of the nation. Between the battles, however, both sides found time to play baseball. Those who knew the game taught it to those who didn't, and when the soldiers returned from the war, they carried the game to hometowns throughout the country. Soon baseball was no longer a leisurely pastime for gentlemen. It became a game for everyone.

Baseball continued to change and grow on the field as well. In 1863, Ned Cuthbert of the Philadelphia Keystones ran from first to second without waiting for a hit—and the stolen base was born. Tom Barlow of the Brooklyn Atlantics invented the bunt, and early bunters used a special small bat that was flattened on one side.

BASEBALL SPREAD LIKE WILDFIRE DURING THE CIVIL WAR, EVEN IN PRISON CAMPS. HERE, IN SALISBURY, NORTH CAROLINA, A UNION PRISONER DASHES FOR SECOND.

"THE SECRET WAS MINE."

—CANDY CUMMINGS (RIGHT) ON HIS NEW "CURVEBALL"

While older boys were away fighting the war, a 14-year-old named Candy Cummings stood at the Brooklyn waterfront, throwing clamshells out over the water. He noticed that the shells curved in the air when he twisted his wrist and wondered if he could do the same

thing with a baseball. Four years later, in 1867, Candy Cummings pitched for the Brooklyn Excelsiors and tried out his curveball. Hitters were completely baffled.

The first professional team—the Cincinnati Red Stockings—was put together by a former New York Knickerbocker named Harry Wright in 1869. That same year, the first transcontinental railroad opened between New York and San Francisco. Wright's team toured the country on the brand-new railroad, bringing high-quality baseball to towns across America.

The Red Stockings' popularity surged as they won 92 games without a loss. Then they had to face the Brooklyn Atlantics, the top team in the East. Over 15,000 fans paid 50 cents apiece to watch the game. Hundreds more climbed trees or peeked through the fence to see the two teams battle it out into extra innings.

Although the Red Stockings lost the game, their success at drawing fans proved that baseball could be a business as well as a sport, and in 1876, the owners of eight professional teams formed the National League of Professional Base Ball Clubs. The League's founder was William Hulbert, owner of the Chicago White Stockings. Hulbert was a ruthless businessman who had made his fortune in the coal business. He regarded the men who worked in his business as parts of a machine, and he felt the same about baseball players.

Under Hulbert's iron-fisted leadership, the National League added a "reserve clause" to the contracts of the five best players on each team.

This meant that the player could play only for that team, year after year, unless the team released or sold him. At first, the players accepted the clause without question; to them it meant they had a job for the next season. But as baseball grew and the reserve clause was extended to all players, they would come to see it for what it was: a form of slavery.

In 1882, a new professional league offered competition to the National League. Officially called the American Base Ball Association, it was nicknamed the "Beer and Whiskey League" because fans could buy alcohol at the ballparks. It was a good time for baseball, with the two league champions meeting in a "World's Series" at the end of the season.

The year the American Association made its debut, William Hulbert died and Albert Spalding took over both the Chicago White Stockings and behind-the-scenes leadership of the National League. A former pitcher, Spalding had left the playing field to start a sporting goods company that manufactured bats, balls, and uniforms. He also made fielding gloves and catcher's masks, but it took him years to convince players to use them. The fans considered it cowardly for a player to wear protective equipment.

"IT IS RIDICULOUS TO PAY BALLPLAYERS $2,000 A YEAR."

—WILLIAM HULBERT, OWNER OF THE CHICAGO WHITE STOCKINGS

ONE OF SPALDING'S LESS SUCCESSFUL IDEAS WAS TO DRESS THE PLAYERS AT EACH POSITION IN DIFFERENT UNIFORMS. THE RESULT WAS CHAOS ON THE FIELD, AND THE EXPERIMENT WAS QUICKLY ABANDONED.

IN THE 19TH CENTURY, BASEBALL CARDS WERE THE ONLY WAY MOST YOUNG FANS COULD SEE WHAT STARS LIKE CAP ANSON LOOKED LIKE.

Spalding promoted the game as if it were a new religion. He led a team of all-stars around the world and published guidebooks about baseball and other sports. Spalding ran his business empire from a private box at the ballpark, with a gong to summon his servants and a brand-new invention—the telephone—to call people who couldn't hear the gong.

Spalding's White Stockings were managed by Adrian C. "Cap" Anson, a powerful, big-talking first baseman. Anson was the greatest hitter of the 19th century, but he hated black people. He was not alone. His attitude reflected a wave of racism that swept the country as whites tried to limit the freedom blacks had gained after the Civil War.

In 1887, when the New York Giants considered signing a black pitcher named George Stovey, Anson made it clear that neither he nor his White Stockings would play against a team with a black player. Rather than face a revolt by their white players, the major league owners arrived at a "gentlemen's agreement": Blacks would not be permitted in organized baseball. Nothing was written down, but the agreement lasted for 60 years.

Although the owners avoided one revolt, they were soon faced with another. In 1890, some of the players formed their own league in rebellion against the hated reserve clause. At first the Players' League was successful, but Spalding and the National League drove it out of business by the end of the season. When the American Association folded a year later, the National League had a monopoly on major league baseball.

By the 1890s, baseball's rules had changed to allow the pitcher to throw overhand. Pitching was becoming a high art. One gangly rookie, in his big-league debut, threw the ball so hard and accurately that the cocky White Stockings were left staring at the bats in their hands. The pitcher's name was Cy Young, and he went on to win 511 games, the most in major league history.

Young once explained why his arm was so strong: "All us Youngs could throw. I used to kill squirrels with a stone when I was a kid, and my granddad once killed a turkey buzzard on the fly with a rock."

"PITCHERS, LIKE POETS, ARE BORN, NOT MADE."

—CY YOUNG (RIGHT)

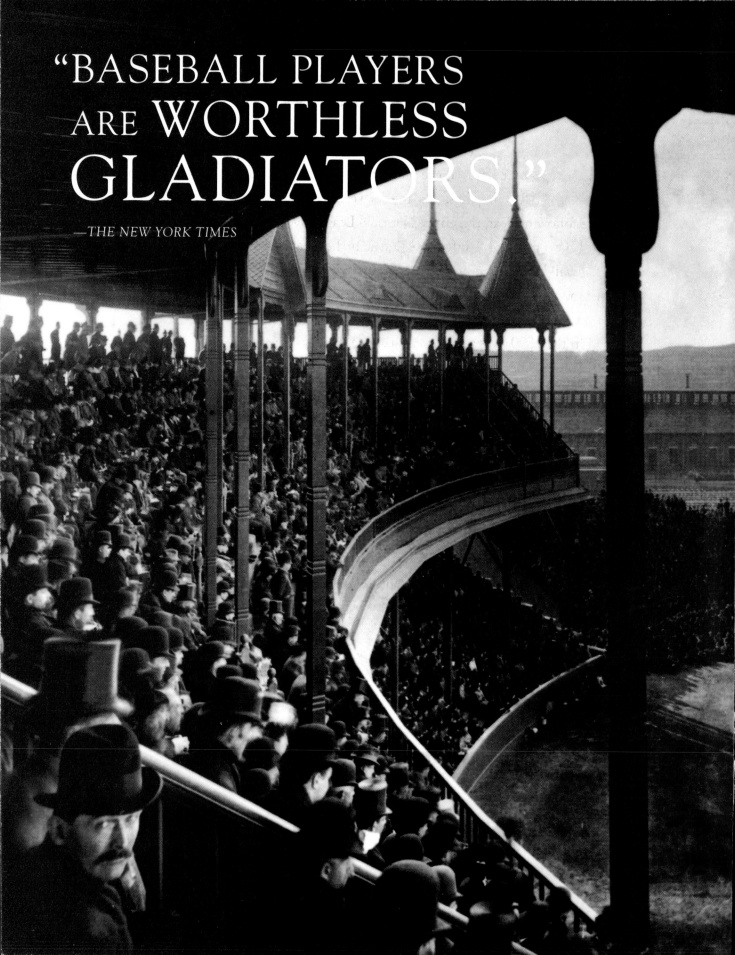

"BASEBALL PLAYERS
ARE WORTHLESS
GLADIATORS."

—THE NEW YORK TIMES

Young was fast, but he wasn't the fastest. Amos Rusie of the New York Giants, "the Hoosier Thunderbolt," threw so hard that his catcher lined his glove with lead to protect his hand. In 1893, in order to give hitters more time to swing at the blazing fastballs of Young and Rusie, the league moved the pitcher's mound back to its present distance of 60 feet 6 inches. The results were immediate and dramatic. The following year, the entire National League averaged over .300, and Boston's Hugh Duffy hit .438, the highest batting average in baseball history. But pitchers soon adjusted to the longer throwing distance and developed tricky pitches, like the spitball and the fadeaway, to regain their edge over the hitters.

Baseball in the 1890s was a rough-and-tumble affair. Players spit tobacco juice into gaping spike wounds and kept on playing. Pitchers scuffed dirt on the baseball to make it do strange things on the way to the plate, and the whole game was often played with one dirty, brown, lopsided ball.

The league was full of tough characters, but no one was tougher than John McGraw, the scrappy third baseman for the Baltimore Orioles. During one game in 1894, McGraw got into a fight with the Boston third baseman. Both benches emptied, the fans joined the brawl, someone set the stands on fire, and the entire wooden ballpark, along with 170 neighborhood buildings, went up in flames.

Although 1890s baseball was wild, the fans began to lose interest. With only one major league, there was no post-season series between league champions. And there wasn't much competition among teams during the regular season. Clergymen and newspapers denounced the rowdy hooliganism of players like John McGraw. Ticket sales dropped, and a national depression made times tight for all businesses, including baseball.

As it looked toward a new century, America's game needed a new beginning. And it was coming in the vision of a man who was so tough himself that a writer once said he looked as if he had been nursed on an icicle.

LEFT: BOSTON BEANEATER FANS AT THE SOUTH END GROUNDS, SOMETIME BEFORE THE 1894 BRAWL THAT LEFT THE WOODEN GRANDSTAND IN A PILE OF ASHES

Ban Johnson was a big man with a big vision. In 1894, he had taken over a minor circuit called the Western League and made it a financial success. In 1900, he changed its name to the American League and began to challenge the National League's control of the professional game.

Johnson promised the fans better, cleaner, and cheaper baseball. He raided the rosters of National League clubs by offering the players higher salaries, and 111 eager National Leaguers, including stars like Cy Young, jumped to Johnson's American League. By 1903, the older league had to accept the wildly successful upstart as an equal partner in major league baseball.

With star players and brand-new teams, the American League brought fresh competition and excitement to the game. On October 1, 1903, the American League champion Boston Pilgrims hosted the National League champion Pittsburgh Pirates in the first game of the first modern World Series, to be played the best five out of nine games. Aided by their wild fans—who taunted Pittsburgh mercilessly—the Pilgrims defeated the favored Pirates five games to three.

It was a great start for the new major leagues, but the next World Series never happened. John McGraw, now the player-manager of the National League champion New York Giants, had been suspended from the American League by Ban Johnson for rowdiness. McGraw was still angry about it, and in revenge, he refused to play the American League champions.

The following year, McGraw's Giants won the National League pennant again, but this time McGraw agreed to play. The Giants easily defeated the Philadelphia Athletics behind the brilliant pitching of Christy Mathewson.

Nicknamed "the Christian Gentleman," Mathewson was clean-living, handsome, well spoken, and college-educated. Schoolboys idolized him, and John McGraw loved him like a son—even though the two men were different in

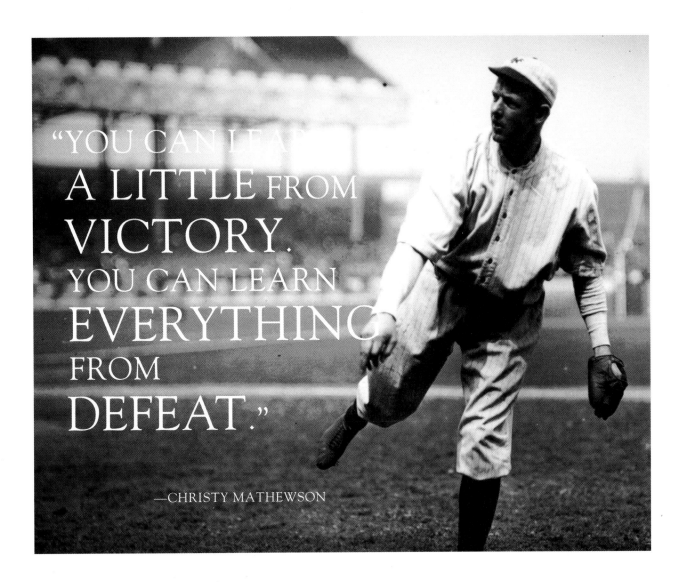

"YOU CAN LEARN A LITTLE FROM VICTORY. YOU CAN LEARN EVERYTHING FROM DEFEAT."

—CHRISTY MATHEWSON

everything except their dedication to winning. Mathewson promised his mother never to play on Sunday, and he never did. But on the other six days of the week, he played with such burning intensity and intelligence that he won 373 games during his career.

Mathewson approached baseball scientifically, cataloging his wide variety of pitches and remembering which pitches worked—or didn't work—against each hitter. He also had a flair for the dramatic. Ten minutes before a game was scheduled to begin, he stepped out onto the field in a long linen coat like those worn by early automobile drivers. Then he walked slowly toward the mound, the crowd cheering louder and louder with every step.

CHRISTY MATHEWSON, STAR PITCHER FOR THE NEW YORK GIANTS. ONE TEAMMATE SAID MATHEWSON COULD THROW A BALL INTO A TIN CUP AT PITCHING RANGE.

If Christy Mathewson was the stately king of the mound, Rube Waddell was the clown prince. A lefty with a blazing fastball and a wicked curve, Waddell led the American League in strikeouts for six straight years. He also led the league in strangeness. He plunged his arm into ice water *before* each game, so he wouldn't "burn up the catcher's glove," and he turned cartwheels when he won. Opponents distracted him with puppies and shiny toys, and Waddell's teammates had to restrain him from running after fire engines while he was pitching.

The early 20th century was an era of great pitchers, and the greatest of them all was a broad-shouldered Kansas farm boy named Walter Johnson. Nicknamed "the Big Train," Johnson threw the ball faster than anyone ever had before. He joined the Washington Senators in 1907 and went on to win 416 games for a team that was usually one of the worst in the league. His record of 110 shut-outs still stands today.

There was one player who could hit Walter Johnson—a young outfielder from Georgia named Tyrus Raymond Cobb. As a teenager, Cobb desperately wanted to prove to his father that he could make it in the major leagues. Then, just before Cobb made his debut with the Detroit Tigers, his mother killed his father with a shotgun. She claimed she had mistaken him for a prowler, but others called it murder. For the rest of his life, Ty Cobb played—and lived—in a constant state of rage.

Cobb viewed everyone else on the field—even his own teammates—as the enemy. He ripped opposing players with sharpened spikes and stormed the stands to beat up fans who heckled him. He was the most hated player in the history of the game; yet he was also its greatest hitter. For 12 seasons, Ty Cobb led the American League in batting. His lifetime average of .367 is the highest in baseball history.

During the early 1900s, the only player who could compete with Ty Cobb for the title of "the greatest ballplayer alive" was Honus Wagner of the Pittsburgh Pirates. Nicknamed "the Flying Dutchman" for his speed on the bases and for his German (*Deutsch*) heritage, Wagner won eight National League batting championships and

"SURE I FOUGHT...
THEY WERE ALL
AGAINST ME."

—TY COBB

TY COBB, WHO BATTED
OVER .300 FOR 23
CONSECUTIVE SEASONS
AND WAS THE GREATEST
BASE STEALER OF HIS
TIME, PLAYED WITH
AN ANGER
THAT LED TO
VIOLENCE BOTH ON
AND OFF THE FIELD.

batted over .300 for 17 consecutive seasons. His talent was as impressive as Cobb's, but his personality was the exact opposite. He treated everyone—even opponents—with good-natured sportsmanship.

In the 1909 World Series, thousands of fans watched eagerly as the two superstars, Honus Wagner and Ty Cobb, faced each other for the first and only time. Wagner was 35; Cobb was 22. The first time Cobb got on base, he yelled down to Wagner at shortstop, "Watch out, Krauthead, I'm coming down! I'll cut you to pieces!"

"Come ahead!" Wagner shouted back. Sure enough, Cobb tried to steal second. Wagner calmly took the throw and tagged him hard on the mouth, splitting his lip.

Honus Wagner went on to outhit and outsteal his younger opponent as the Pirates edged the Tigers four games to three. After the Series, Cobb said admiringly, "That Dutchman is the only man in the game I can't scare."

"BASEBALL…IS NO PINK TEA, AND MOLLYCODDLES HAD BETTER STAY OUT."

—TY COBB

SPECTATORS AT PITTSBURG

DURING THE 1909 WORLD SERIES, BOISTEROUS PITTSBURGH FANS CLIMB A LAMPPOST TO CHEER THEIR TEAM ON.

Across America, millions followed the 1909 World Series in newspapers and on special scoreboards that displayed every hit and every out. Baseball was still the rough-and-tumble game it had been in the 1890s, but it had reached new heights of competition and excitement.

Convinced that baseball was an original American game, sporting goods king Albert Spalding formed a committee in 1905 to discover how baseball began. Two years later the committee reported that an American schoolboy named Abner Doubleday—who later became a heroic general in the Civil War—had invented the game at Cooperstown, New York, in 1839. The report was not true, but Spalding wanted to believe it, and America wanted to believe it with him.

In a single decade, baseball—and players like Christy Mathewson, Ty Cobb, and Honus Wagner—had recaptured the imagination of the American people. It looked as if nothing could stop baseball now. Except maybe baseball itself.

GENTLEMEN AND BLACK SOX.
From the beginning, baseball had been at war with itself. Was it a "gentleman's game" that represented the highest American ideals? Or was it a game for the toughest of the toughs—men like John McGraw and Ty Cobb—a game where all that mattered was winning? Or was it something worse—a game where all that mattered was winning unless someone paid you more to lose?

On Opening Day of the 1910 season, for the first time in history, a U.S. president—William Howard Taft—threw out the first ball. Taft weighed over 300 pounds and required a special chair in the presidential box at the ballpark. The President spoke for most Americans when he called baseball "a clean, straight game."

Connie Mack, manager and part-owner of the Philadelphia Athletics, also believed that baseball should be clean. The son of an Irish millworker, Mack was not a gentleman by birth, but he dressed and acted like one. He managed in a business suit rather than a baseball uniform, and he forbade his players to use obscene language or insult their opponents.

DIGNIFIED CONNIE
MACK PREACHED
GENTLEMANLY
CONDUCT ON
AND OFF
THE FIELD.

"THERE IS ROOM FOR GENTLEMEN IN ANY PROFESSION."

—CONNIE MACK

Led by Mack, the Athletics dominated the first half of the decade, winning four pennants and three world championships. But their success ultimately led to their downfall. Rather than pay the players the higher salaries they deserved for winning, Connie Mack broke up the team after the 1914 season. Being a gentleman was one thing; business was another.

Mack's penny-pinching reflected the war that raged at the heart of baseball—the war between the players and the owners. In 1912, the frustrated players organized the Fraternity of Professional Base Ball Players of America. The Fraternity had two goals: to get rid of the reserve clause and to gain a greater share of the profits from their labor.

Seeing that many players were dissatisfied, a group of wealthy businessmen formed the Federal League in 1914. The new league offered players an opportunity to change teams, forcing the two older leagues to agree to some of the players' demands—or lose their stars. Since the 19th century, the owners had charged the players rent for their uniforms. Now the owners agreed to pay for the uniforms and to paint the outfield fences dark green so the batters could see the ball better. They also raised the salaries of star players. Ty Cobb jumped from $12,000 to $20,000 a year.

Despite their early promise, the Federal League and the Fraternity of Professional Base Ball Players collapsed, leaving the players back where they began, with no power and no control over their careers.

Baseball survived the war within the game, but in the spring of 1917, it was faced with a real war—World War I. Teams learned military drills and proudly marched with bats on their shoulders to the delight of patriotic fans. Although the owners tried to keep their players out of the war, 227 major leaguers served in the armed forces. Three died in action, and others returned forever scarred by their wartime experiences.

LED BY FRANKLIN DELANO ROOSEVELT, THEN ASSISTANT SECRETARY OF THE NAVY, THE WASHINGTON SENATORS PARADE ACROSS THE FIELD TO SHOW THEIR READINESS FOR WORLD WAR I.

Christy Mathewson inhaled poison gas during a training exercise and permanently damaged his lungs. He never pitched again, and died seven years later. Star pitcher Grover Cleveland Alexander served with an artillery unit. He came back shell-shocked, half-deaf, and drinking heavily to forget the horrors he'd seen.

By 1919, baseball was back to normal—at least on the playing field. But a new threat was brewing off the field, a scandal so great that it would shake the faith of the entire nation.

It began with Charles Comiskey, the miserly owner of the Chicago White Sox (formerly the White Stockings). Once a player himself, Comiskey was so cheap that he paid his players half what others were earning on lesser teams. He even refused to pay for his players' uniforms to be washed. In 1918, out of protest, the team had played in uniforms so dirty that they called themselves the "Black Sox." The name would soon take on a more sinister meaning.

Despite the team's problems, the White Sox powered to the top of the American League in 1919. They were heavily favored to defeat the Cincinnati Reds in the World Series, to be played the best out of nine games. But before the Series began, Chicago first baseman Chick Gandil arranged with a small-time gambler to lose the Series in return for $100,000—a fortune at the time. Gandil was nearing the end of his career, and he figured this was his last chance to make some real

money. Seven other Chicago players joined the conspiracy, including star pitchers Eddie Cicotte and Lefty Williams and slugger Shoeless Joe Jackson.

A South Carolina country boy who could neither read nor write, Jackson had earned his nickname when he played a minor league game in socks because his shoes were too tight. He swung a huge 48-ounce bat named "Black Betsy" and carried a parrot that could squawk only two words: "You're out!" Like Christy Mathewson before him, Shoeless Joe was idolized by schoolboys across America.

On the second pitch of the first game of the 1919 World Series, Eddie Cicotte hit the Cincinnati leadoff man right between the shoulder blades. That was a signal to the gamblers: The fix was on.

Chicago lost four of the first five games, riddled by obviously poor pitching and strange fielding errors. But then the tide began to turn. The gamblers had not come up with all the money they'd promised, so the conspirators decided to forget the deal. They won the next two games, with Lefty Williams scheduled to pitch Game Eight. The night before the game, a Chicago thug known as "Harry F." visited Williams and threatened to hurt him and his wife if he lasted past the first inning. The next day, Williams gave up three quick runs and was yanked in the first. Cincinnati went on to win the game—and the Series.

CROWDS FOLLOW THE ACTION IN THE 1919 WORLD SERIES, TRANSMITTED BY TELEGRAPH TO AN AUTOMATED SCOREBOARD IN TIMES SQUARE, NEW YORK CITY.

"THEY AREN'T HITTING. DON'T KNOW WHAT'S THE MATTER."

KID GLEASON, WHITE SOX MANAGER

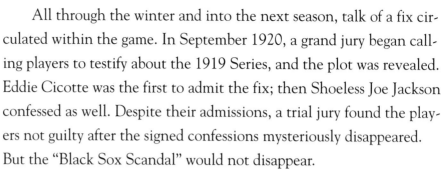

All through the winter and into the next season, talk of a fix circulated within the game. In September 1920, a grand jury began calling players to testify about the 1919 Series, and the plot was revealed. Eddie Cicotte was the first to admit the fix; then Shoeless Joe Jackson confessed as well. Despite their admissions, a trial jury found the players not guilty after the signed confessions mysteriously disappeared. But the "Black Sox Scandal" would not disappear.

Baseball had battled gambling since the early days, but to fix the World Series was to attack the very heart of the national pastime. During the trial—in an attempt to restore the game's integrity— the desperate team owners had appointed federal judge Kenesaw Mountain Landis as the first Commissioner of Baseball and given him complete control over the major leagues.

The day after the jury's decision, Landis banished the eight Chicago players from baseball for life. His decisive action helped restore the average fan's faith in the American game. But it would take a player—a moon-faced mountain of muscle named George Herman Ruth—to bring back the thrill.

RAND JURY HAS YET TO REACH BIG MEN IN GAME'S SCANDAL

Indictment of Eight White Sox Players Only One Phase of Inquiry That Judge McDonald Says Will Continue Until There Is Real Cleanup.

EVELOPMENTS IN BASEBALL INQUIRY

Eight White Sox players, on confessions made by several of them, are indicted for conspiracy to their part of fixing the 1919 World's Series. Those indicted:

Chick Gandil   Swede Risberg
Eddie Cicotte   George Weaver
Claude Williams   Fred McMullin
Joe Jackson   Oscar Felsch

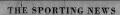

FIX THESE FACES IN YOUR MEMORY

"CHICK" GANDIL

"HAP" FELSCH   JOE JACKSON

EDDIE CICOTTE

CLAUDE WILLIAMS   FRED McMULLIN   "SWEDE" RISBERG   "BUCK" WEAVER

EIGHT MEN CHARGED WITH SELLING OUT BASEBALL

WHEN BASEBALL GETS BEFORE THE GRAND JURY

CINCINNATI THINKS BRIBE MONEY WASTED

STILL BELIEVES REDS WOULD HAVE WON IN HONEST SERIES.

Natural Reason for Moran's Men Not Being Tipped Off That Games Would Be Given Away.

CINCINNATI, O., Oct. 4.—

ED CICOTTE CROSSED HIS DETROIT FRIENDS

TOLD THEM WHITE SOX HAD CINCH IN WORLD'S SERIES.

Nemo Leibold Refused to Answer Letter of Inquiry and Now the Reason for It Comes Out.

DETROIT, Mich., Oct. 4.—

"I'M FOREVER
BLOWING BALL GAMES,
PRETTY BALL GAMES
IN THE AIR."

— JOURNALIST RING LARDNER, WHO TAUNTED THE BLACK SOX WITH
HIS VERSION OF "I'M FOREVER BLOWING BUBBLES"

George Herman Ruth Jr. grew up fast on the rough waterfront of Baltimore, Maryland. The son of an Irish saloonkeeper, Ruth was stealing from local shops at the age of five. By seven he was chewing tobacco and refusing to go to school, despite brutal beatings by his father. Finally his parents sent him to a reform school and orphanage called St. Mary's Industrial School for Boys. There, young Ruth discovered something that changed his life forever. He discovered baseball.

In 1914, at the age of 19, Ruth left St. Mary's to play professional baseball and was soon pitching for the Boston Red Sox. After all his years in reform school, he acted like an animal released from a cage—eating and drinking everything in sight, spending every penny he earned. His teammates called him "Baby," and then just "Babe."

For six seasons, during the finest years of the Red Sox, Babe Ruth was the best left-handed pitcher in the American League, winning 89 games and setting a World Series mark of 29⅔ consecutive scoreless innings. But Ruth could do more than pitch—he could wallop the ball like no one had ever walloped it before. His soaring home runs seemed to fly forever, and the fans loved it. In 1919, Ruth smashed a record 29 homers.

BABE RUTH, ALSO KNOWN AS "THE BAMBINO" AND "THE SULTAN OF SWAT," CLOUTS ANOTHER.

But that was only the beginning. In January 1920, the Red Sox sold Ruth to the New York Yankees for $125,000, the largest sum ever paid for a ballplayer up to that time. For the Red Sox, it was the end of an era—and, some say, the start of a curse. They had won three World Series with Ruth; to this day, they have not won another. For the Yankees, however, it was the beginning of a dynasty. During the next 15 years, Babe Ruth, home runs, and the New York Yankees would dominate major league baseball and fire the imagination of the American people.

Seeing how fans loved the home run, the owners made some changes in the game around the time that Ruth was sold to the Yankees. They began to use a new wool from Australia inside the ball. It was "livelier" and could be wound tighter than the old wool, making the ball travel farther. The owners also outlawed marking, scuffing, or spitting on the ball. Then, in the middle of the 1920 season, a tragedy forced one more change.

On August 16, Yankee pitcher Carl Mays hit Cleveland shortstop Ray Chapman in the head with a rising fastball. As usual, the ball was dirty and hard to see. Chapman died the next day, the first and only fatality in a major league baseball game. To help batters see the ball better, umpires were instructed to put a new ball in play as soon as the

"I HIT BIG OR I MISS BIG. I LIKE TO LIVE AS BIG AS I CAN."

—BABE RUTH

old one got dirty. The worn, "dead" ball of the past was now a clean, new, "live" ball. Baseball became a hitter's game.

When he joined the Yankees, Ruth left pitching behind and became a full-time slugger. During his first year in New York, he pounded out 54 home runs. The next year, he walloped 59 homers and led the Yankees to their first American League pennant. Fans came out in record numbers to see him, and in 1923, the Yankees built a brand-new stadium to accommodate them. Over 74,000 people—the largest crowd up to that time—watched Babe christen "the House That Ruth Built" with a massive blast on Opening Day.

"SOME BALL YARD!"

BABE RUTH ON YANKEE STADIUM.

APRIL 18, 1923:
OPENING DAY AT
YANKEE STADIUM.
AT THE TIME, IT
WAS THE LARGEST
BALLPARK IN THE
COUNTRY.

For the first time in baseball history, one player stood head and shoulders above the rest. Ruth loved every minute of it. He earned the highest salary in baseball and made thousands more advertising everything from cigarettes to soap. He drank whiskey before breakfast, stuffed down half a dozen hot dogs for lunch, and changed silk shirts seven times a day. He drove fancy cars and posed with politicians, and found friendly ladies in every town—which didn't make his wife very happy.

Then, at the beginning of the 1925 season, Ruth's wild living caught up with him. He collapsed with stomach pains and required emergency surgery. His illness was never explained. American papers reported he had just eaten too many hot dogs, washed down with too many soda pops. They called it "the Bellyache Heard 'Round the World."

While Babe Ruth was igniting major league baseball, black baseball was coming into its own. Although black teams had been around since before the Civil War, there had never been a top-level professional league for black players. Then, in 1919, a visionary black promoter named Andrew "Rube" Foster formed the Negro National League for the 1920 season. Foster was a former pitcher who had earned his nickname by defeating the great lefty Rube Waddell in an exhibition game.

RUBE FOSTER

Foster's league became a huge success, drawing over 400,000 fans in 1923. Seeing the potential for profit, a group of white businessmen formed a rival league, the Eastern Colored League. The following year, the two league champions met in the first Negro World Series. Sadly, Rube Foster broke down under the strain of keeping his league together. Believing he was about to be called to pitch in the white World Series,

HARD TIMES, GOOD TIMES.

In 1930, during the early days of the Great Depression, Babe Ruth signed a contract for $80,000 a year. When asked if he thought it was right for a ballplayer to make more than the President of the United States, the Babe replied, "Why not? I had a better year than he did."

Worse years were on the way. By 1932, almost one out of every three workers was out of a job. Company presidents jumped out of windows. Desperately poor people sold apples on the street. It was hard to find 50 cents to go to the ballpark.

Faced with the hard times of the Great Depression, team owners tried new gimmicks. On July 6, 1933, the greatest major league players squared off at Chicago's Comiskey Park in the first All-Star Game. Babe Ruth, the biggest all-star of them all, led the American League to victory with a two-run blast and a game-saving catch.

That same year, Larry MacPhail, the general manager of the Cincinnati Reds, decided to broadcast Cincinnati games on the radio. Games had been broadcast before, but they were seldom "live" from the ballpark, because most owners believed radio would take away from attendance at the park. MacPhail knew they were wrong—and he was right. Radio created whole families of fans who wanted to go and see the stars they heard about in their living rooms.

MacPhail had another idea, too—night baseball. At a time when Americans were scrambling desperately to keep any job they had, most people couldn't take off work during the day to see a ball game. So MacPhail had lights installed at Cincinnati's Crosley Field. On May 24, 1935, the Reds and Philadelphia Phillies played the first night game in major league history. Within 10 years, every team except the Chicago Cubs would install lights in its stadium.

In St. Louis, Cardinals general manager Branch Rickey was also taking a creative approach to the game. Even before the hardships of the Depression, Rickey began his own "farm system" of minor league teams to find and develop players for the majors. He was a brilliant judge of talent, and his farm system produced many great players for the Cardinals and other teams. But the greatest product of Rickey's farm system— and the most entertaining—was the 1934 Cardinals, known as the Gashouse Gang.

The team earned its nickname the day after a muddy double-header. Too broke to pay for laundry, they played in uniforms so dirty that a reporter said they looked like the grimy workers for the local gas company. Dirty or not, the Cardinals won the world championship with a scrappy, all-or-nothing brand of baseball that echoed the earlier style of John McGraw and Ty Cobb. To many Americans, they embodied the qualities that kept the country going during the Great Depression: toughness, hard work, and a sense of humor.

The Gashouse Gang boasted the wildest assortment of characters since the days of Rube Waddell. Third baseman Pepper Martin put sneezing powder in the air vents of hotels, and played in spite of a broken finger, casually pointing out that it was "only a small bone." Second baseman–manager Frankie Frisch got so upset over bad calls that he jumped up and down on his cap until his spikes ripped it to shreds. But the gassiest guy of the gang was a lanky right-hander from Arkansas named Jay Hanna "Dizzy" Dean.

"THEY X-RAYED MY HEAD AND FOUND NOTHING."

—DIZZY DEAN AFTER BEING HIT BY A BALL IN THE 1934 WORLD SERIES

Dean, who proclaimed himself "the greatest pitcher in the world," dropped out of school in second grade—and admitted that he "didn't do too well in first grade, either." In his prime, Dean averaged an impressive 24 wins a year and entertained fans and players alike with a steady stream of brash banter. When facing a new batter, Dean would ask, "Son, what kind of pitch would you like to miss?"

Some of the most creative baseball during the 1930s, however, was played *outside* the majors—by the black athletes who still weren't welcome in the white baseball world. The Eastern Colored League had collapsed in 1928, and Rube Foster's Negro National League folded in 1931. But black teams continued to play independently, and in 1933, the Negro National League reemerged, financed by black gamblers, the only people in the black community who had the necessary money during the Depression.

Black baseball was a sight to see: fast and flexible, beautiful and brilliant. With Babe Ruth, white baseball had become a slower game, relying more and more on the home run. A player would hit a single and wait for someone to drive him in with a towering blast. Black players didn't wait for anything. They'd get to first on a walk or a bunt, dance off the bag to drive the pitcher crazy, steal second, go to third on a bunt or a grounder, and even steal home.

The most famous black player was pitcher Satchel Paige, a skinny string bean so full of hot air and humor that he made the Gashouse Gang look like a bunch of shy librarians. After Paige defeated Dizzy Dean in an exhibition game, Dizzy admitted Paige was the greatest pitcher he'd ever seen. Satchel agreed. He claimed to have pitched 2,500 games during his career and won 2,000 of them. Paige had special names for his pitches: the bee ball, jump ball, trouble ball, and midnight rider. Batters said they were just different words for *fast*.

Black teams played wherever and whenever they could—in stadiums and farmers' fields—two, three, four games a day. Six years before Larry MacPhail brought lights to the majors, the black Kansas City Monarchs were carrying portable lights on trucks to bring in the after-supper crowd. In northern cities, black players stayed at fine

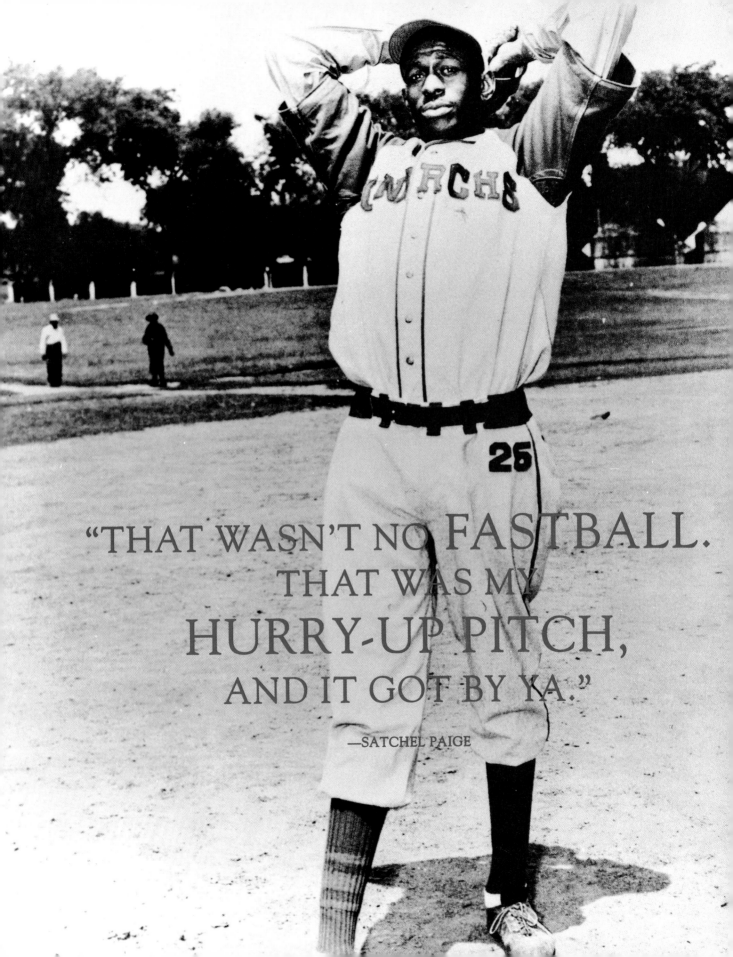

"THAT WASN'T NO FASTBALL.
THAT WAS MY
HURRY-UP PITCH,
AND IT GOT BY YA."

—SATCHEL PAIGE

AS EARLY AS 1929, THE
KANSAS CITY MONARCHS
WERE DRAWING
AFTER-SUPPER CROWDS
WITH PORTABLE
FLOODLIGHTS, WHICH
THEY CARRIED FROM
TOWN TO TOWN
ON SPECIAL
FLATBED TRUCKS.

black-owned hotels and ate at fine black-owned restaurants. In the South, they had to sleep in railroad stations under police guard and eat in alleyways.

Black players packed major league stadiums—while the white teams were away—and delighted fans across the country. In off-season exhibitions, black teams played white teams at least 438 times. The black teams won 309 of those games. Buck O'Neil, who played first base for the Kansas City Monarchs, later offered an explanation for this incredible record: "The major league ballplayers were just trying to make a payday. But we were trying to prove to the world that we were as good or better."

"AND WE WON. WON LIKE WE INVENTED THE GAME."

—A PITTSBURGH CRAWFORDS TEAM MEMBER

While black baseball boomed, white baseball marked the end of an era when Babe Ruth retired in 1935. Then, in the spring of 1939, Yankee powerhouse Lou Gehrig abruptly took himself out of the lineup after 2,130 consecutive games. Although only 35 years old, he was stumbling around like an old man and would die two years later of an incurable illness now called Lou Gehrig's disease.

As the Roaring Twenties faded into memory, the 1930s brought new ideas that sent baseball hurtling into the future. One of the best new ideas was a celebration of the past. On June 12, 1939, the Baseball Hall of Fame opened in Cooperstown, New York, the mythical birth-place of the game. Thirteen baseball greats were inducted into the Hall that day, including Babe Ruth, Ty Cobb, Honus Wagner, Cy Young, Walter Johnson, and Christy Mathewson.

The old heroes of the game were passing. But new heroes were already stepping onto the field to take their place.

THE FIRST INDUCTEES TO THE HALL OF FAME. STANDING *(LEFT TO RIGHT):* HONUS WAGNER, GROVER CLEVELAND ALEXANDER, TRIS SPEAKER, NAPOLEON LAJOIE, GEORGE SISLER, WALTER JOHNSON. SEATED *(LEFT TO RIGHT):* EDDIE COLLINS, BABE RUTH, CONNIE MACK, CY YOUNG. NOT PHOTOGRAPHED: CHRISTY MATHEWSON AND WILLIE KEELER, WHO HAD BOTH DIED, AND TY COBB, WHO CAME LATE TO THE CEREMONY.

BREAKING THE BARRIER. By the spring of 1941, Hitler had conquered Western Europe and was preparing to invade Russia. The Japanese army occupied large areas of China and Southeast Asia. Every day brought America closer to the time when young men would carry guns and hand grenades instead of bats and balls. But then—like the calm before a storm— baseball had one last glorious season.

LEFT:
DODGER FANS
LINE UP FOR A
1941 WORLD
SERIES GAME.

HERE,
A WORLD WAR II
SAILOR RELAXES
AT A GAME IN
BROOKLYN'S
EBBETS FIELD.

On May 15, 1941, Joe DiMaggio hit a single at Yankee Stadium. This wasn't particularly surprising. He hit lots of singles. Lots of home runs, triples, and doubles, too. Now in his sixth season with the Yankees, DiMaggio was already hailed as "the next Babe Ruth."

But what happened after the single was more than surprising—it was amazing. DiMaggio got a hit in the next game. And the next. And the next. Ten games. Twenty games. Thirty games. As the streak continued, people all over America—even people who didn't care about baseball—began to follow DiMaggio's progress with fascination and delight. "Did he get one?" they'd ask, and everyone knew exactly what they were talking about.

JOE DIMAGGIO LINES A SINGLE TO LEFT FIELD TO CONTINUE HIS INCREDIBLE HITTING STREAK.

"DIMAGGIO EVEN LOOKS GOOD STRIKING OUT."

—TED WILLIAMS

On June 29, in the first half of a doubleheader, DiMaggio tied the American League record by hitting in 41 consecutive games. Before the second game, a fan reached down from the stands and stole his favorite bat. But that didn't stop DiMaggio. He borrowed a bat and stroked a single. On July 5, he pounded a three-run homer to break the all-time record of 44 games. Three days later, he got his bat back from a young fan who had tracked it down in New Jersey. "Joltin' Joe" celebrated by smashing another homer. Finally, on July 17—two months and two days after it began—Joe DiMaggio's incredible hitting streak ended at 56 games.

Now baseball fans began to follow another young slugger, Ted Williams of the Boston Red Sox. Intense, proud, and moody, Williams approached the art of hitting with single-minded devotion. "All I want out of life," he said, "is that when I walk down the street folks will say, 'There goes the greatest hitter that ever lived.'"

Going into the last day of the season, Williams' batting average was .39955, which would be officially rounded up to .400. No one had batted over .400 in 11 years. But Williams wanted to do it without any "rounding up."

As the first game began, Williams was so nervous that his hands shook. But he smashed a single down the first-base line. It was the first of six hits that afternoon—four singles, a double, and a home run—in eight trips to the plate. Williams reached his goal and then some, finishing the season with a batting average of .406. In all the years since, no major leaguer has batted .400 again. And no one has approached Joe DiMaggio's 56-game hitting streak.

A ST. LOUIS POSTER FOR A BROWNS–YANKEES GAME CAPITALIZES ON DIMAGGIO'S STREAK.

RED SOX SLUGGER TED WILLIAMS (IN UNIFORM) DIDN'T LIKE REPORTERS, AND THE FEELING WAS MUTUAL. "I NEVER MET YOU BEFORE," WILLIAMS TOLD ONE SPORTSWRITER, "BUT YOU'RE NO GOOD. NO GOOD TILL YOU PROVE OTHERWISE."

Two months after the 1941 World Series, Japanese planes bombed Pearl Harbor and the United States entered World War II. President Franklin Delano Roosevelt—a baseball fan himself—requested that the major leagues continue during the war, although players of draft age would have to serve in the armed forces.

DURING WORLD WAR II, U.S. SOLDIERS IN EUROPE RELAX WITH A GAME OF BASEBALL— DESPITE INCOMING ENEMY FIRE.

One of the first players to enlist was Detroit Tiger slugger Hank Greenberg, who had challenged Babe Ruth's home run record in 1938, belting out 58 homers. Greenberg, who was Jewish, later said that every home run felt like a blow against Hitler, who was already persecuting Jews in Germany.

With stars like Greenberg, Joe DiMaggio, and Ted Williams in the armed forces, teams scrambled to fill their rosters with older players, younger players, and players who were physically unfit for service. World War II major league baseball was sloppy, but it was still baseball, and fans came out to the park to relax from the tension and hard work of the war years.

In the Midwest, Philip Wrigley, owner of the Chicago Cubs, created the All-American Girls Professional Baseball League to offer small-town fans a fresh form of baseball entertainment. Women's teams had been around since the 19th century, but Wrigley's league was by far the most successful experiment, drawing over a million fans in its best year. On and off the field, the players were supposed to act like "ladies"—one player was even called back to the dugout because she forgot to wear lipstick. But the women played tough, exciting baseball that delighted fans and impressed professional baseball men.

Pitcher Jean Faut threw two perfect games, and slugger Joanne Weaver hit .429 one season. Sophie Kurys, nicknamed "Tina Cobb," stole 201 bases in a single season and was thrown out only twice.

Olympia Savona was so talented that it was said, "She runs bases like a man, slides like a man, and catches like a man. If she could spit, she could go with Brooklyn."

By 1946, the war was over and major league baseball was back to normal—and for over 60 years, "normal" had meant no black players. But that was about to end.

Branch Rickey, already famous for establishing the farm system, was now running the Brooklyn Dodgers. He decided the time had come for a more important change. A deeply religious man, Rickey believed that integrating baseball was the right thing to do. He also believed it made good business sense. He knew that black players would bring fans—black and white—to the ballpark and make the Dodgers a stronger team on the field.

On August 29, 1945, Branch Rickey met with Jackie Robinson, a brilliant shortstop for the Kansas City Monarchs. Rickey never used profanity, but for three hours he shouted every racist insult he could think of to show Robinson what might be in store for him as a major league player. Robinson was a proud man with a quick temper, and the

SOPHIE KURYS OF THE RACINE BELLES WAS NICKNAMED "TINA COBB" FOR HER SPEED AND DARING ON THE BASES.

"IF SHE COULD SPIT, SHE COULD GO WITH BROOKLYN."

—UNNAMED SPORTSWRITER, DESCRIBING OLYMPIA SAVONA

insults infuriated him. Rickey explained that he needed a man with the courage not to fight back. A single violent incident on the field could set the cause of integration back 20 years.

Jackie Robinson thought long and carefully. Finally he promised that he would not fight back; he would just play baseball.

On April 15, 1947—after a year in the minors—Jackie Robinson trotted out onto the field for the Brooklyn Dodgers, the first black man ever to play in the National League. It was a cold, rainy afternoon, and 15 photographers surrounded him, taking his picture from every possible angle. Of the 26,623 fans at Ebbets Field, half were African Americans, who greeted Robinson's every move with enthusiasm and joy. White fans cheered him too, shouting, "Jackie! Jackie! Jackie!" That day, Robinson went 0 for 4, but it didn't matter. The barrier had been broken. The "gentlemen" no longer agreed.

Despite his Opening Day reception, Robinson faced a long, difficult season. He endured a steady stream of insults and death threats to himself and his family. Opposing players tried to injure him, and some of his own teammates refused to speak to him at first. Although it tore him apart inside, Robinson kept his promise to Branch Rickey. He did not fight back; he just played baseball. And Robinson's style—the fast-paced, creative, "tricky baseball" of the Negro leagues—set attendance records all over the league.

That year, Jackie Robinson batted .297, with 29 stolen bases and 12 home runs, as he helped lead the Dodgers to the 1947 National League pennant. Considering the pressure and abuse that he faced, it was one of the most extraordinary performances in baseball history. A few months earlier, The Sporting News had doubted Robinson's ability to compete against major league players. Now the paper selected him as its first Major League Rookie of the Year.

Other black people called Jackie Robinson a "race man," because he represented the hopes and pride of African Americans. He was not only a champion baseball player, he had opened the door for other great black players who would raise America's game to new heights. Finally, baseball was truly the national pastime.

"BASEBALL PEOPLE ARE GENERALLY ALLERGIC TO NEW IDEAS."

—BRANCH RICKEY

JACKIE ROBINSON
BROUGHT THE
FAST-PACED, "TRICKY"
STYLE OF THE NEGRO
LEAGUES TO THE
MAJORS. HERE HE
STEALS HOME—ONE
OF 19 TIMES IN
HIS CAREER.

ON THE MOVE. In the fifties, many Americans left the old eastern cities for neatly manicured suburbs and a distant dream in the West. Powerful cars and brand-new highways took them where they wanted to go. And when they got there, a magic box called television brought the sights and sounds of baseball into their homes. Attendance at the old ballparks fell dramatically. But where the people of America went, baseball would soon follow.

In 1951, *all three* New York teams finished in first place. The Yankees won the American League pennant for the third year in a row. The excitement was in the National League, where the New York Giants and Brooklyn Dodgers tied for first, forcing a three-game playoff to determine the winner. New Yorkers were riveted to their tiny black-and-white television screens as the Dodgers and the Giants each won a game, and the whole season came down to one last battle at the Polo Grounds. In the bottom of the ninth inning, the Dodgers led 4–1, but the Giants made a thrilling comeback, capped by Bobby Thomson's three-run blast down the left field line. Newsreels called it "the Shot Heard 'Round the World."

The World Series couldn't match the excitement of the playoffs. The Yankees steamrolled over the Giants four games to two for their third consecutive world championship under manager Casey Stengel. In previous managing jobs, Stengel had been considered a loser and a clown, famous for antics like fainting when he didn't like an umpire's call. When he took over the Yankees in 1949, however, Stengel stopped fainting and started winning. But he kept his upbeat personality and unique mangling of the English language.

"I made up my mind, but I made it up both ways," Stengel once explained—which didn't explain anything. In spring training, he would order his players to "line up alphabetically according to your height." Perhaps his greatest, yet most confusing, wisdom was that "good pitching will always stop good hitting, and vice versa."

Despite his strange way with words, Casey Stengel had a brilliant mind for baseball. He got the most out of his pitching staff by using relief pitchers more frequently than other managers up to that time. And he got the most out of his hitters by platooning: playing right-handed hitters against left-handed pitchers, and left-handed hitters against righties, in order to give his batters the best view of the breaking ball. Stengel had learned platooning as a player for John McGraw; today, it's standard baseball strategy.

Stengel had another strategy that he once explained in his own unique way: "I never play a game without my man." Stengel's "man"

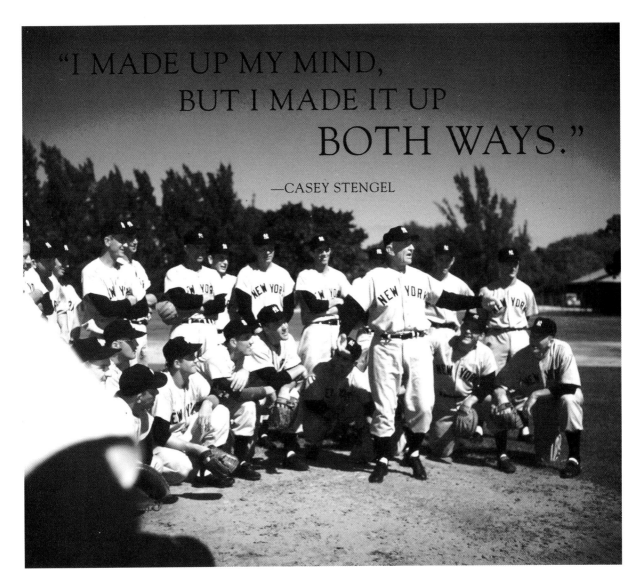

"I MADE UP MY MIND,
BUT I MADE IT UP
BOTH WAYS."

—CASEY STENGEL

was Yogi Berra, a ham-fisted, pug-faced son of an Italian bricklayer from St. Louis. At first Yankee fans thought Berra was too odd-looking and clumsy to be a "true" Yankee. But Berra worked hard, and with Stengel's instruction, he became one of the greatest catchers in baseball history, winning the Most Valuable Player Award three times.

Berra not only shared Stengel's dedication to the game; he also shared his way with words. "You can see a lot just by observing," he once pointed out. Later, when he became a manager himself, Berra offered his classic take on a tight pennant race: "It ain't over till it's over."

"BASEBALL IS 90 PERCENT MENTAL. THE OTHER HALF IS PHYSICAL."

—YOGI BERRA

Under Casey Stengel, the Yankees dominated the decade, winning eight American League pennants and six World Series. But though the Yankees were almost unstoppable as a team, fifties' baseball had more great individual stars than any decade before or since. Many came from the Negro leagues, which struggled and ultimately collapsed as their stars left one by one. But the steady stream of great black players raised the major league game to a new level of brilliance and competition.

In 1949, Jackie Robinson was chosen the Most Valuable Player in the National League. Over the next decade, eight out of 10 National League MVP Awards also went to former Negro league players. Catcher Roy Campanella, Robinson's Brooklyn teammate, won three. Slugging shortstop Ernie Banks of the Chicago Cubs won two. The others went to Brooklyn pitcher Don Newcombe, Milwaukee Braves outfielder Hank Aaron, and a young center fielder for the New York Giants named Willie Mays.

Mays entered the league in 1951, just four years after Jackie Robinson had opened the door. But those four years had already made a difference in racial attitudes. As Mays explained, "All the Negro players who came up to the majors before I did had the same scouting report. First, they said the player was a Negro, and then they said he was great. With me they said great, then they said Negro."

Giants manager Leo "the Lip" Durocher once said that there were five things a baseball player could do: hit, hit for power, run, field, and throw. Willie Mays could do them all brilliantly. He batted over .300 for his career, hit 660 home runs, led the league four times in stolen bases, and played center field like a magician, purposely wearing a cap a size too big so it would fall off as he made spectacular catches.

Across the Harlem River in Yankee Stadium, another young center fielder, Mickey Mantle, could also do it all. The son of a poor Oklahoma lead miner, Mantle could smash the ball with awesome power from either side of the plate, including one tape-measure blast

WILLIE MAYS SMASHES A HOME RUN. WHEN MAYS ENTERED THE LEAGUE FOUR YEARS AFTER JACKIE ROBINSON, HIS ABILITY AND SHOWMANSHIP QUICKLY MADE HIM A STAR.

that carried over 600 feet. But he wasn't just a power hitter; before injuries damaged his legs, Mickey Mantle was the fastest man in baseball.

Mantle, Mays, Hank Aaron, and Ernie Banks represented another trend of the fifties—the dominance of the slugger. Ever since Babe Ruth, baseball fans had carried on a love affair with the home run—and the owners wanted to give them what they loved. In 1950, the Rules Committee made the strike zone smaller in an effort to increase home run production. It worked. Throughout the fifties and early sixties, major league players hit more home runs than ever before.

But fans weren't coming out to the ballparks as often as they had in the past. Branch Rickey, who had moved on to run the Pittsburgh Pirates, blamed television. "Radio created a desire to see something,"

TELEVISION CAMERAS BROUGHT MAJOR LEAGUE BASEBALL INTO AMERICAN LIVING ROOMS. HERE, THE BROADCASTER AT THE MIKE IS FORMER GASHOUSE GANG PITCHER DIZZY DEAN.

he explained. "Television is giving it to them. Once a television set has broken them of the ballpark habit, a great many fans will never acquire it."

But there were other reasons, too. The dominance of New York teams was great for New York, but it wasn't much fun for fans in other cities. And many of the old ballparks were falling apart, along with the neighborhoods around them. Middle-class Americans—who had been the most loyal fans—were moving away from the old cities, out into the suburbs and west to California.

BROOKLYN DODGER
FANS PROTEST THEIR
BELOVED TEAM'S
DEPARTURE FOR
THE WEST.

As they did, cities like Boston, St. Louis, and Philadelphia could no longer support two major league teams. In 1953, the Boston Braves moved to Milwaukee, the first major league franchise to change cities in 50 years. In 1954, the St. Louis Browns became the Baltimore Orioles, and the Philadelphia Athletics moved to Kansas City. Finally, in 1958, even New York could no longer support all three teams, and the Dodgers and Giants left for California—breaking the hearts of their remaining fans.

It was the end of an era. During the next decade, baseball and America would enter the space age, and the major league game would stretch from coast to coast.

TED WILLIAMS
HITS ONE LAST
HOME RUN OUT
OF FENWAY
PARK.

On a cold, windy September day in 1960, Ted Williams stepped to the plate for the last time. This extraordinary hitter had played major league ball in four different decades. But now he was 42, too old to play his best, and he had decided to retire.

In the eighth inning, facing a pitcher who had not even been born when Williams broke into the league, the great hitter launched a towering drive for his 521st home run. Williams circled the bases quickly, unsmiling, with his head down—just as he had done for the last two decades. When his teammates pleaded with him to go out and tip his hat to the cheering fans, Williams refused. He hadn't acknowledged the crowd for 20 years, ever since some fans booed him during his second season. He would not do it now.

There would never be another Ted Williams—a man who hit with a magical mix of precision, power, and pride. But it was still the age of the slugger. In 1961, Yankee teammates Mickey Mantle and Roger Maris assaulted one of the game's greatest records: Babe Ruth's 60 home runs. Injuries ultimately forced Mantle out with 54 homers, but Maris just kept going. Finally, on the last day of the season, he blasted number 61 into the right field bleachers at Yankee Stadium.

In 1927, Babe Ruth had said, "Let's see some other [guy] do that!" Now some other guy *had* done it. But he had done it in eight more games. That season, the American League had added two new teams and expanded its schedule from 154 to 162 games. Baseball experts still argue whether Maris "truly" broke Ruth's record. Maris himself almost cracked from the media attention and the strain of chasing the game's most beloved hero. Toward the end of his life, he told a friend, "It would have been a lot more fun if I had never hit those sixty-one home runs. All it brought me was headaches."

The year after Maris broke Ruth's record, major league hitters pounded over 3,000 homers—almost twice what they averaged in the late 1940s. Fearing that the balance between hitters and pitchers was out of control, the Rules Committee expanded the strike zone back to its original size. Around the same time, pitchers developed a new weapon called the slider, which looked like a fastball but broke down and away just as it reached the plate. And night baseball—more popular than ever—made it harder to see the ball. A golden age of pitching began.

MARIS WATCHES HIS 61st HOMER FLY INTO THE RIGHT FIELD BLEACHERS BEFORE TAKING OFF AROUND THE BASES.

"PITCHING IS THE ART OF **INSTILLING FEAR** BY MAKING A MAN **FLINCH.**"

—SANDY KOUFAX

There were many great hurlers during the sixties: Bob Gibson, Don Drysdale, Whitey Ford, Denny McLain. But perhaps the greatest of all was Dodger lefty Sandy Koufax. For five years, from 1962 through 1966, Koufax dominated hitters. He led the National League in earned run average every year, pitched four no-hitters, including one perfect game, and won 111 games while losing only 34. He won three Cy Young Awards—given to the best pitcher in baseball—and one MVP Award while leading the weak-hitting Dodgers to three pennants and two world championships. And he did it while pitching in constant pain from a damaged elbow that required him to take painkillers and cortisone shots in order to play.

In 1966, Koufax won 27 games—the most by a National League lefty in the 20th century. Only 30 years old, he was at the top of his career and the highest-paid player in the game. But he retired at the end of the season. It wasn't the pain in his elbow that stopped him; it was the medication he had to take in order to play. "I don't know if cortisone is good for you or not," he explained. "But to take a shot after every other ball game…and to be high half the time during a ball game because you're taking painkillers…I don't want to have to do that." Five years later, Sandy Koufax became the youngest player elected to the Hall of Fame.

The sixties was an age of expansion, as baseball reached out to new fans in new cities. Eight teams were added, including the Montreal Expos of Canada, the first major league team outside the United States. In 1969, the major leagues were divided into two divisions each. Playoffs, called the League Championship Series, would be held to determine the two pennant winners.

New ballparks rose and old ballparks crumbled to the ground. The most amazing new stadium was Houston's Astrodome, where baseball moved indoors. To many Americans, the arching, air-conditioned dome represented a miracle of space-age technology. When the grass died for lack of sunlight, it was replaced with a synthetic carpet called Astroturf. Today, 10 major league stadiums use artificial turf, which has led to new plays, new strategies, and a faster-paced game.

DESPITE A PRICE TAG OF $31.6 MILLION, THERE WERE PROBLEMS AT THE HOUSTON ASTRODOME. THE GRASS DIED, AND THE LUCITE DOME MADE IT IMPOSSIBLE FOR PLAYERS TO SPOT A FLY BALL. THE ANSWERS: ASTROTURF AND A PAINT JOB.

"IF THE HORSES WON'T EAT IT, I WON'T PLAY ON IT."

—PHILADELPHIA INFIELDER DICK ALLEN, ON ASTROTURF

All of the new teams were pretty bad at first, but the worst of the bunch was the New York Mets. When they entered the league in 1962, Casey Stengel came out of retirement to manage them, but even "the Ol' Perfesser" couldn't teach them how to play. They looked more like a comedy act than a baseball team: bumping into each other, dropping balls, and winding up with too many men on a base. Met first baseman "Marvelous Marv" Throneberry was once called out after hitting a triple because he forgot to touch first base. When Stengel stormed out of the dugout to argue, the umpire said, "I hate to tell you this, Casey, but he missed second base, too."

But no matter how badly the Mets played, their fans loved them. When the Giants and Dodgers deserted New York, they left behind legions of brokenhearted fans who couldn't bear to root for the rival Yankees. Instead, they adopted the Mets as their own, and throughout the sixties, the lowly Mets brought in more fans than the Yanks. Then, in 1969, the Mets *really* gave their fans something to cheer about.

The team started out the season as usual, losing seven of its first 10 games. Oddsmakers made the Mets a 100–1 shot to win the '69 pennant. But then something amazing happened: The Mets began winning… and winning…and winning. They won the Eastern Division, and rolled over the Atlanta Braves in the

ANOTHER ERROR FOR THE NEW KIDS ON THE BLOCK, AS METS INFIELDERS ROY McMILLAN *(LEFT)* AND CHUCK HILLER GO FOR THE SAME FLY BALL. McMILLAN FINALLY CAUGHT IT—AND DROPPED IT.

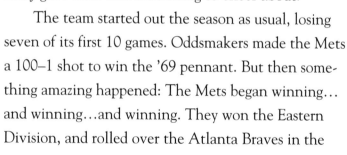

"I SEE NEW WAYS TO LOSE I NEVER KNEW EXISTED BEFORE."

—CASEY STENGEL, ON HIS AMAZIN' METS

first-ever National League Championship Series. In the World Series, they faced the Baltimore Orioles, one of the most powerful teams of all time, led by slugger Frank Robinson and third baseman Brooks Robinson. No one gave the Mets a chance.

Before the 1969 season, the Rules Committee had lowered the pitching mound and shrunk the strike zone again, because they were afraid that pitchers had become too dominant. But the Mets' young pitching staff was so good that they dominated anyway, handcuffing the hard-hitting Orioles to take the Series in five games. Their fans celebrated by ripping up the outfield grass, and New York City treated its heroes to a ticker-tape parade through the streets of Manhattan. The Amazin' Mets had become the Miracle Mets.

While the Mets were celebrating their World Series victory, Curt Flood, the star center fielder of the St. Louis Cardinals, was informed that he had been traded to the Philadelphia Phillies. Flood didn't want to go. But he was bound by the reserve clause in his contract. He had two choices: play for the Phillies or not play at all. Flood decided to fight for a better choice—and his fight would change baseball forever.

THE AMAZIN' METS AND THE CHICAGO CUBS SCRAMBLE FOR FIRST PLACE IN THE 1969 PENNANT RACE.

FREE AGENTS AND MILLION-DOLLAR MEN. On Christmas Eve of 1969, Curt Flood wrote a letter to Baseball Commissioner Bowie Kuhn. "Dear Mr. Kuhn," it began. "After 12 years in the Major Leagues, I do not feel that I am a piece of property to be bought and sold irrespective of my wishes." Flood vowed to challenge the reserve clause all the way to the U.S. Supreme Court. He did. And he lost the battle. But the players would win the war.

When Curt Flood's case was heard in federal court, no active players spoke on his behalf. They were all too afraid of the owners. Hank Greenberg spoke for Flood, and so did former team owner Bill Veeck. The most eloquent testimony came from Jackie Robinson, his hair white and his body aged by diabetes and heart disease. Despite their support, Flood lost his case. But he had done what he believed was right. And for the first time, the average fan began to wonder: Maybe the reserve clause really was a form of slavery.

In 1973, Atlanta Braves slugger Hank Aaron fought his own battle for respect and dignity as he approached Babe Ruth's lifetime record of 714 home runs. A dozen years earlier, Roger Maris had nearly cracked under the strain of chasing Ruth. But Maris was white and a Yankee. Aaron was neither. He received almost a million pieces of mail that year—much of it filled with racist insults and violent death threats. More than 25 years after Jackie Robinson broke the color barrier, racism was alive and well in America—and in America's game.

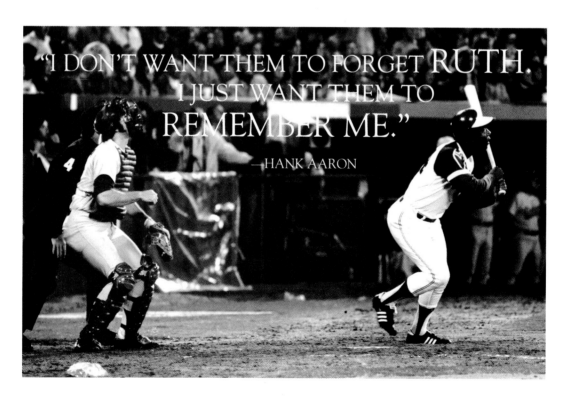

"I DON'T WANT THEM TO FORGET RUTH. I JUST WANT THEM TO REMEMBER ME."

—HANK AARON

A strong-willed, quiet man, Aaron ended the season one home run short of Ruth's record. He blasted number 714 on Opening Day of 1974, and broke the record a few days later. In 1976, Hank Aaron retired with 755 career home runs. He was the last man still playing in the majors who had once played in the Negro leagues.

Despite thrilling performances by players like Aaron, baseball suffered during the early seventies. Attendance fell, especially in the American League, which added the designated hitter in 1973, allowing a player to bat for weak-hitting pitchers. Many fans—as well as many talented athletes—were drawn to faster-moving sports like football and basketball. Baseball had once seemed a lightning-fast game for a rapidly growing America. But now America was moving faster than ever, and the old game of baseball seemed slow.

Owners tried crazy gimmicks and promotions to bring in the fans, from dancing chickens to instant replays on huge screens in the parks. To attract younger fans, Charles Finley of the Oakland A's paid his players bonuses to grow fashionably long hair, beards, and mustaches. The hairy A's won the world championship three years in a row—from 1972 to 1974—with great stars like Reggie Jackson, Catfish Hunter, and Vida Blue. But they still struggled to draw fans.

Then, in 1975, came a World Series that reminded America what baseball was all about. The Boston Red Sox and Cincinnati's "Big Red Machine" were strong teams with many colorful characters, and they battled neck and neck through a thrilling seven-game Series. Seventy-five million people watched the final game on television, the largest viewing audience for a sporting event up to that time.

Two months after the 1975 Series, the reserve clause finally died. When Curt Flood lost his case in the courts, Marvin Miller, the hard-fighting leader of the Major League Players' Association, looked for another way to challenge the clause. He found it in two key words: *one year*. The clause stated that if a player and owner could not agree on a new contract, the player had to play for the same team under his old contract for one more year. The owners had said this meant they could keep the player year after year. But Miller said that one year is one

year—and *only* one year. After that, a player would become a free agent, with the right to play for any team. This time the courts backed him up.

The owners claimed that free agency would be the death of baseball. It wasn't, but it did change the game in some important ways. For years fans had rooted for their favorite players on their favorite teams, until the players and the team became one and the same: Joe DiMaggio and the New York Yankees; Ted Williams and the Boston Red Sox; Jackie Robinson and the Brooklyn Dodgers. Now star players could move from team to team, selling their services to the highest bidder. And the richest teams could hire the best players.

With free agency, player salaries grew higher and higher until—for the first time in history—the best players made more money than some of the men who owned the teams, and by the 1990s the average player salary was over $1 million. But the owners did not give up without a struggle. During the eighties, baseball was torn by player strikes and a secret plot by the owners to simply refuse to hire free agents. It was similar to the old "gentlemen's agreement," but this time the plot was uncovered by Miller and the Players' Association, and the owners were forced to pay the players $280 million in lost wages. Times had definitely changed.

Yet the more things changed, the more they stayed the same. For over 20 years, Pete Rose had played a tough, hustling style of baseball that reminded older fans of Ty Cobb. He hit like Cobb, too—year after year after year. Finally, on September 11, 1985, Rose stroked a single into left-center field at Cincinnati's Riverfront Stadium to pass Cobb's all-time hit record. A Goodyear blimp flying above the stadium flashed the message in giant letters: "Pete Rose, 4,192."

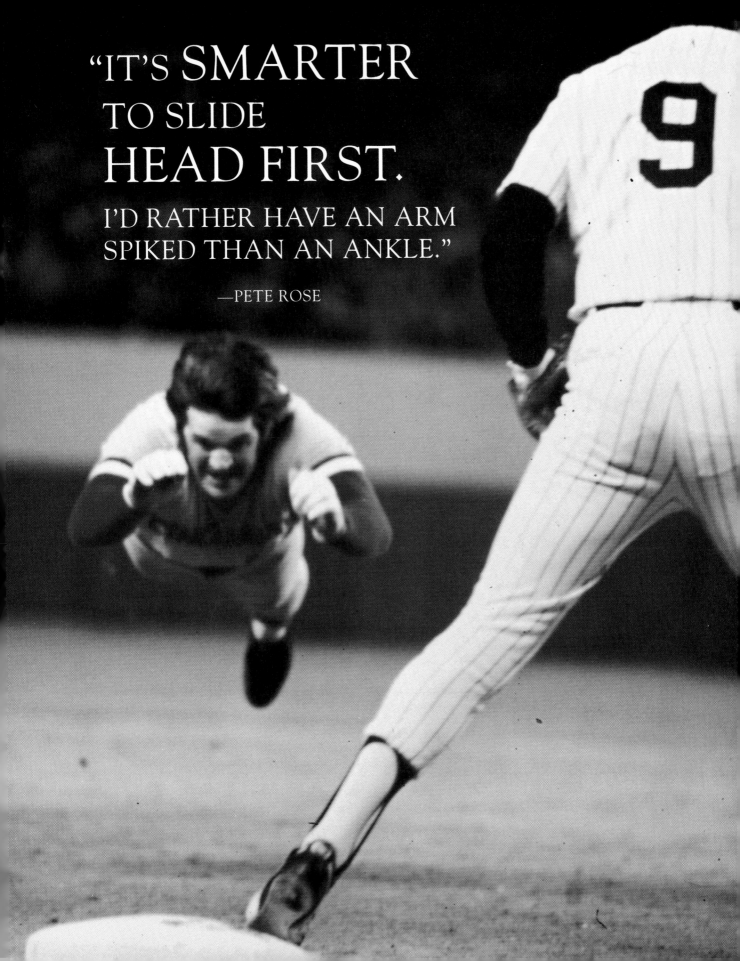

"IT'S SMARTER
TO SLIDE
HEAD FIRST.
I'D RATHER HAVE AN ARM
SPIKED THAN AN ANKLE."

—PETE ROSE

Rose went on to get 4,256 hits before retiring in 1986, but he stayed in the game as the Reds' manager. Then, in 1989, Baseball Commissioner A. Bartlett Giamatti banned Rose from baseball for life. Rose was accused of gambling on baseball games—a charge that he denied. Ironically, Ty Cobb had once been suspended for gambling, but his suspension was lifted, and he was allowed to return to the game. Unless Pete Rose's suspension is lifted, the man with the most hits in baseball history cannot enter the Hall of Fame.

The Pete Rose scandal tore apart the world of baseball and disappointed fans across the country. But Rose is only one of many players who have fallen from grace because of personal problems.

Gambling, alcoholism, and drug use have all tarnished America's game. Baseball players may be heroes on the field, but they are human—and human beings make mistakes. Yet in the end, it is the heroics we remember.

In the 1988 World Series, something happened that was as miraculous as anything in the long history of the game. The powerful Oakland A's were heavily favored over the Los Angeles Dodgers. In the ninth inning of Game One, the A's were leading 4–3, and the Dodgers were batting with two outs and one man on. Desperate for a run, Dodger manager Tommy Lasorda asked Kirk Gibson if he could pinch-hit. Gibson had been the Dodgers' best hitter all season, but he had injured both legs and could barely walk. Grunting in pain, he took some practice swings and said, "I think I've got one good swing in me."

Like a wounded warrior, Gibson limped out to face Dennis Eckersley—the finest relief pitcher in baseball. Gibson fouled off two quick strikes. Then he watched three pitches miss the plate, working the count to 3 and 2 as he waited for his one good swing. Finally, Gibson slammed an Eckersley slider into the 10th row of the right field bleachers—and the Dodgers won, 5–4. As Gibson limped around the bases, the Dodger dugout exploded in joy, and the A's stared toward the bleachers in disbelief. The Dodgers went on to beat the A's in five games.

It was the only time Kirk Gibson batted in the Series, but he made his mark on America's game with a single swing.

That's baseball.

"THE ST___ OF LE__END."

—SPORTSCASTER _OB COSTAS __ K__ _IBSON PREPARED TO PINCH-HIT

INDEX

Page numbers in **boldface** refer to illustrations.

Aaron, Hank, 61, 62, **74**, 74-75
Alexander, Grover Cleveland, 28, **47**
All-American Girls Professional Baseball League, 52-53
All-Star Game (1933), 42
American Base Ball Association, 11, 13
American League, 16, 18, 75
Anson, Adrian C. "Cap," 12, **12**
artificial turf, 69
Atlanta Braves, 70-71.
    See also Boston Braves

Baltimore Orioles (early franchise), 15
Baltimore Orioles (modern franchise), 63, 71
Banks, Ernie, 60, 62
Barber, Red, **42**
Barlow, Tom, 9
Baseball Hall of Fame, 47, **47**
Berra, Yogi, 58-60, **60**
Black Sox Scandal, 28-30, **31**
Blue, Vida, 75
Boston Beaneaters, **14**, 15
Boston Braves, 63.
    See also Atlanta Braves
Boston Pilgrims, 18
Boston Red Sox, 34-35, 75, 76
Brooklyn Atlantics, 10
Brooklyn Dodgers, **49**, 54, 55, 58, 63, **63**, 70, 76.
    See also Los Angeles Dodgers

Campanella, Roy, 60
Cartwright, Alexander Joy, 8
Chapman, Ray, 35
Chicago Cubs, 42, **71**
Chicago White Sox, 28-30
Chicago White Stockings, 10, 11, 12, 13
Cicotte, Eddie, 28, 29, 30
Cincinnati Reds, 28, 29, 42, 75
Cincinnati Red Stockings, 10
Civil War, 9
Cobb, Tyrus Raymond "Ty," 20, **21**, 22-23, 24, 27, **28**, 43, 47, 76, 78, **78**
Collins, Eddie, **47**
Comiskey, Charles, 28
cricket, 8
Cummings, Candy, 10, **10**
Cuthbert, Ned, 9

Dean, Jay Hanna "Dizzy," **43**, 43-44, **62**
Dempsey, Jack, 32
designated hitter, 75
Detroit Tigers, 20, 22-23
DiMaggio, Joe, **50**, 50-51, **51**, 52, 76
domed stadiums, 69, **69**
Doubleday, Abner, 6
Drysdale, Don, 68
Duffy, Hugh, 15
Durocher, Leo, 61

Eastern Colored League, 37, 44
Eckersley, Dennis, 78
Evers, Medgar, 64

farm system, 42
Faut, Jean, 52
Federal League, 27
Finley, Charles, 75
fixed games, 28-30, **31**
Flood, Curt, 71, 72, **73**, 74, 75
Ford, Henry, 16
Ford, Whitey, 68
Foster, Andrew "Rube," **37**, 37-38, 44

Fraternity of Professional Base Ball Players of America, 26, 27
free agency, 75-76
Frisch, Frankie, 43

gambling, 78
Gandil, Chick, 28
Gehrig, Lou, **38**, 38-39, **39**, 47
Giamatti, A. Bartlett, 78
Gibson, Bob, 68
Gibson, Kirk, 78-79, **79**
Great Depression, 40, 42, 43, 44
Greenberg, Hank, 52, 74

"Harry F.," 29
Hiller, Chuck, **70**
Hitler, Adolf, 48, 52
Huggins, Miller, **37**
Hulbert, William, 10-11
Hunter, Catfish, 75

Jackson, Reggie, 75
Jackson, Shoeless Joe, 28, 30, **30**
Johnson, Ban, 16, 18, **18**
Johnson, Walter, 20, 47, **47**

Kansas City Monarchs, 44, **46**
Kennedy, Bobby, 64
Kennedy, John F., 64
King, Martin Luther, Jr., 64
Koufax, Sandy, 68, **68**
Kuhn, Bowie, 72
Kurys, Sophie, 52, **53**

Lajoie, Napoleon, **47**
Landis, Kenesaw Mountain, 30
Lasorda, Tommy, 78
Lindbergh, Charles, 32
Los Angeles Dodgers, 68, 78-79.
    See also Brooklyn Dodgers

McGraw, John, 15, 18-19, 24, 43, 58
Mack, Connie, 26, **26**, **47**
McLain, Denny, 68
McMillan, Roy, **70**
MacPhail, Larry, 42, 44
Major League Players' Association, 75-76
Malcolm X, 64
Mantle, Mickey, 62, 66
Maris, Roger, 66-67, **67**, 74
Martin, Pepper, 43
Mathewson, Christy, 18-20, **19**, 23, 28, **28**, 47
Mays, Carl, 35
Mays, Willie, 61, **61**, 62
Merriwell, Frank (fictional character), **17**
Miller, Marvin, 75-76
Montreal Expos, 69

National Association of Base Ball Players, 8-9
National League Championship Series (1969), 70-71
National League of Professional Base Ball Clubs, 10-11, 13, 15, 18
Negro National League, 37-38, 44
Newcombe, Don, 61
New York Giants, 12, 18, 58, 63, 70
New York Knickerbocker Base Ball Club, 8, **8**
New York Mets, 64, **70**, 70-71, **71**
New York Yankees, 35, 36, 38-39, 58-60, **59**, 70, 76
night games, 42, 67

Oakland Athletics, 75, 78-79.
    See also Philadelphia Athletics
O'Neil, Buck, 46

Paige, Satchel, 44, **45**
Philadelphia Athletics, 18, 26, 63.
    See also Oakland Athletics

Philadelphia Phillies, 42, 71
Pipp, Wally, 38
Pittsburgh Pirates, 18, 22-23
platooning, 58
Players' League, 12-13

racial integration, 53-54, 60-61
racism, 12, 74
radio, games on, 42, 62
records:
    base hits, career, 76, 78, **78**
    base hits in consecutive games, **50**, 50-51, **51**
    batting average, career, 20
    games won, pitcher, career, 13
    home runs, career, **74**, 74-75
    home runs, season, 39, 52, 66-67, **67**
    shut-outs, career, 20
reserve clause, 10-11, 12, 26, 71, 72, 74, 75-76
Rickey, Branch, 42, 53-54, 62
Robinson, Brooks, 71
Robinson, Frank, 71
Robinson, Jackie, 53-54, **55**, 60, 61, 74, 76
Roosevelt, Franklin D., **27**, 52
Rose, Pete, 76, **77**, 78, **78**
rounders, 8
Rusie, Amos, 15
Ruth, George Herman "Babe," 30, 32-39, **33**, **34**, **37**, **38**, **39**, 40, 42, 44, 47, **47**, 50, 52, 62, 66, 67, 74, 75

St. Louis Browns, 63
St. Louis Cardinals, 42-44, 71
Savona, Olympia, 53
Sisler, George, **47**
Spalding, Albert, 11-12, 13
Speaker, Tris, **47**
The Sporting News, **31**, 54
Stengel, Casey, 58, 59, **59**, 60, 70
Stovey, George, 12
Super Chicken, **75**

Taft, William Howard, 26
television, games on, 56, 58, 62, **62**, 75
Thomson, Bobby, 58
Throneberry, "Marvelous Marv," 70
Tip Top Weekly, **17**
town ball, 8

Valentino, Rudolph, 32
Veeck, Bill, 74

Waddell, Rube, 20, 37, 43
Wagner, Honus, **22**, 22-23, 47, **47**
Washington Senators, 20
Weaver, Joanne, 52
Williams, Lefty, 28, 29
Williams, Ted, 51, **51**, 52, 66, **66**, 76
women's baseball, 52-53
World Series:
    of 1903, 18, **18**
    of 1905, 18
    of 1909, 22-23, **23**
    of 1919, 28-30, **29**
    of 1941, **49**
    of 1951, 58
    of 1969, 64, 71
    of 1975, 75
    of 1988, 78-79, **79**
World War I, **27**, 27-28
World War II, 48, **49**, 52, **52**
Wright, Harry, **8**, 10
Wright, Orville, 16
Wrigley, Philip, 52

Young, Cy, 13, 15, 18, 47, **47**